Hay

Landscape,
Literature
& the Town
of Books

Seren is the book imprint of
Poetry Wales Press Ltd
Nolton Street, Bridgend, Wales

www.serenbooks.com
facebook.com/SerenBooks
Twitter: @SerenBooks

© Jim Saunders, 2014

The right of Jim Saunders to be identified
as the Author of this Work has been asserted
in accordance with the Copyright, Designs
and Patents Act, 1988.

ISBN 978-1-78172-178-0

A CIP record for this title is available from the British Library

All rights reserved. No part of this publication
may be reproduced, stored in a retrieval system,
or transmitted at any time or by any means
electronic, mechanical, photocopying, recording
or otherwise without the prior permission
of the copyright holders.

The publisher works with the financial assistance
of the Welsh Books Council

Printed by Akcent Media Ltd, in the Czech Republic

HAY

Landscape, Literature and the Town of Books

Jim Saunders

SEREN

If the writer should at all appear to have induced any of his readers to pay a more ready attention to the wonders of the Creation, too frequently overlooked as common occurrences; or if he should by any means, through his researches, have lent an helping hand towards the enlargement of the boundaries of historical and topographical knowledge; or if he should have thrown some small light upon ancient customs and manners, and especially on those that were monastic; his purpose will be fully answered. But if he should not have been successful in any of these his intentions, yet there remains this consolation behind – that these his pursuits, by keeping the body and mind employed, have, under Providence, contributed to much health and cheerfulness of spirits, even to old age; and, what still adds to his happiness, have led him to the knowledge of a circle of gentlemen whose intelligent communications, as they have afforded him much pleasing information, so, could he flatter himself with a continuation of them, would they ever be deemed a matter of singular satisfaction and improvement.

                        Gilbert White: *The Natural History of Selborne*, 1788

Hay time above Hay

Winter at the Warren

Contents

Introduction	9
What did the Romans do for Hay?	11
Hay People – Pete Dorling	16
The Buildings of Hay	18
The Other Twin Towers	26
Hay Castle	29
Hay People – Alan Powell	37
An Excursion to the Black Mountains	39
On the Black Hill	53
Hay People – Joyce Gervis	62
The Hay Festival	67
Hay People – Max Pfefferkorn	76
Chapel	78
Hay People – Kirsty Williams	84
Kilvert and Clyro	87
An Excursion to Bettws Clyro	94
Hay People David Eckley	98
Dandelion Dead	100
The Wye	103
Hay People – Johnny Golesworthy	109
An Excursion with Alfred Watkins	112
On the Trail of the Lonesome Pine	118
Hay People – Sara Bowie	120
Holmes and the Hound	122
Hay People – Josie Pearson	128
An Excursion with the Woolhope Naturalists'22 Field Club	130
In Search of Owain Glyndŵr	132
An Excursion to Monnington-on-Wye	140
An Excursion along the Offa's Dyke Path	144
The Kissing Bridge	150
The Brecon Beacons	154
Bibliography	158

None of the other new Border castle towns was as successful as Ludlow, and although places such as Hay on Wye, Knighton and Montgomery enjoyed a modicum of prosperity, today they carry an air of detached obscurity.

Trevor Rowley: *The Landscape of the Welsh Marches*, 1986

Introduction

I first came to Hay in 1987, when researching a job application. Clearly it was the right thing to do, because I got the post, as Offa's Dyke Path Officer. It was the job I had always wanted and it became my mission for the next 18 years. The Path goes right through the middle of Hay so I had plenty of opportunities to visit the town, for site meetings, to erect footbridges, signposts and stiles, and, when not working, to drink coffee at the Granary and attend the Hay Festival.

So when I was commissioned to write *Offa's Dyke – a journey in words and pictures* in 2006 I knew enough about Hay to include a little discourse on the town and its literary connections.

It was at the Hay Festival that I had the idea to enlarge that discourse into another book. Perusing the Festival's bookshop one day it struck me that among all the weighty volumes there was nothing specifically on Hay. Having worked for some years as a volunteer driver for the Festival I had observed how people enjoyed the whole Hay experience. It was not just about the books, or even the town, but the people, the setting, the landscape, the sense of being somewhere different, the buzz. So I thought I'd put that in a book. A little bit of Hay to take away. Did I succeed? Let me know: critics@bookofhay.co.uk

One other thing: Hay-on-Wye is not in Herefordshire, it is in Wales. Cusop is another matter but Hay is in Wales. Its postal address is Hereford, but Hay is in Wales. And its Welsh name is Y Gelli Gandryll. Now read on.

Hay in May

This was in the Olden Days, when the Romans were top nation on account of their classical education, etc.

1066 and ALL THAT

What did the Romans do for Hay?

Hay is a Norman town, created in the twelfth century, long after the Romans left Britain. So what *did* the Romans do for Hay? Well they had two forts just across the Wye, where Boatside Farm stands today, and they also had a town at Kenchester, about five miles west of modern Hereford. Evidently they needed to get from one to the other because they built a road, which is still in use today. Two thousand years later most people travelling from Hay to Hereford still cross the river to Clyro and, from there, follow the A438, which is the route of the Romans.

But there were people about here even before the Romans, and a little digging turns up a surprising amount of evidence of this. In 1959 and 1960 the pupils of Clyro Court Seconday School (now the Baskerville Hall Hotel) found over two hundred flint arrowheads and tools at Old Forest Farm in Clyro. A report of this in the 1961 *Transactions of the Radnorshire Society* says:

> The occurrence of a large number of flint implements and flakes in such a small area is strong evidence for the existence of some sort of settlement at Old Forest, probably during the late neolithic period.

For neolithic read 'New' Stone Age. Also of the Stone Age is a chambered tomb close by the entrance to Clyro Court and, further afield, Arthur's Tomb at Bredwardine, over the border in Herefordshire. Archaeologists reckon the latter to be as many as 5,000 years old.

Pen y Beacon stone circle

South of the town, on the summit of Hay Bluff there is a Bronze Age burial cairn and on the plateau below it another, more substantial, burial mound as well as the remains of a stone circle.

While the Romans penetrated deep into Wales, building roads and forts and mining for minerals, the Saxons had less success. In the late eighth century, they built Offa's Dyke, probably to mark the line of their furthest advance. We'll come back to that later.

Whereas King Offa marked out his territory with a bank of earth (albeit a very impressive one) three centuries on the Normans marked theirs with castles and towns. Here is Trevor Rowley on the subject:

> By 1110 the army of Bernard de Newmarche had overrun the whole of the Dark Age Welsh princedom of Brycheiniog. In his wake three new towns, Brecon, Builth and Hay were created.

and

> Both Builth and Hay also retain clear indications of their Norman origins in their street plans, and it is reasonable to assume in all three cases that they were laid out within a few years of the building of their castles.

A brief study of the Ordnance Survey (OS) map quickly reveals why the site of Hay might have been chosen, both for a castle and for a town. Not only does it command the valley of the Wye, a strategic route into Wales, but it stands opposite a spur of raised ground which constrains the course of the river, making a good location for a bridge.

Norman motte,
Swan Bank, Hay

Once castles arrived they multiplied. Within a five mile radius of Hay the OS map shows castle sites at Hay, Clifford, Clyro and Cusop (two). Further mottes or mottes and baileys are shown at Hay, Llanigon, Llowes, Cwrt Evan Gwynne (Clyro), Newton Tump (Clifford), and Dorstone (two). These are not necessarily all of the same period of course but they do suggest a history of conflict over a wide area.

Famously South Wales was completely transformed in the nineteenth century by the Industrial Revolution, but in the border country around Hay change was far more subtle. The arrival of the railway gave farmers easier access to distant markets but it did not bring the rapid urban expansion which followed in other parts of the country. Neither does it seem to have brought a flood of cheap imported building materials, as happened elsewhere. A perambulation of the town will reveal plenty of slate roofs and some shiny red Ruabon Brick, both from North Wales, but there is still lots of local stone on show. (Actually Richard Haslam reports that many of the nineteenth century frontages in High Town conceal seventeenth century timber-framed houses.)

So right up to the late twentieth century Hay remained a predominently rural, agricultural town, described by Rowley, in 1986, as having "an air of detached obscurity". Not so much now though.

So, a short history of Hay: Stone Age, Bronze Age, Ancient Britons, Romans, (Saxons), Normans, (Owain Glyndŵr), railways, roads, bookshops, Metropolitan Media Types.

Local stone; the Granary Restaurant at the clock

Shiny red Ruabon brick, in Broad Street

Hay People – Pete Dorling, Archaeologist

A walk with Pete Dorling is full of surprises. This is the sort of conversation you will have:

"That's Bronze Age burial cairn"
"What is?"
"What you are standing on"

Thus when we were driving up to Hay Bluff one sunny but bitter February day, in search of historic house platforms, he pointed to a mound on the left of the road and said "That's Twyn y Beddau" and told me a story about a practical joke played on Victorian archaeologists conducting a dig there in Francis Kilvert's time. Now I have driven that road dozens of times and never even noticed the mound right beside it. Shame on me.

In 2014 Pete was working for the Herefordshire Archaeology Service, but previously he had been Archaeologist for the Brecon Beacons National Park, which is how I came to know him. Years ago we walked the Offa's Dyke Path over the Black Mountains and he opened my eyes to a whole new world. He has lived in and around Hay for more than 25 years but, like me, was a Buckinghamshire boy originally. His son has worked for Joyce Gervis's Ty-Mawr Lime. Everyone tends to know everyone around here.

His favourite book? *Passage to Juneau: A Sea and its Meaning* by Jonathan Raban, about sailing, history, autobiography, landscape and loss.

Pete Dorling on Twyn y Beddau

And at Pen y Beacon stone circle

Richard Haslam's Hay

Left. *"The vicarage on its E, built apparently as late as c. 1840 as the George Inn, has a pedimented doorcase in its five-bay front and on the r. its own stable and archway."*

Opposite: *"Two distinct elements of Hay are the pleasing mesh of streets and alleys on the slopes of its fortress precinct, and its modest provincial early C19 classicism in warm grey stone, at the SW particularly."*

The Buildings of Hay

In 1951 Penguin Books published the first volume of their celebrated series 'The Buildings of England' by German architectural historian Nikolaus (later Sir Nikolaus) Pevsner. The series eventually covered the whole of that country, one county at a time. The twenty-fifth volume, *Herefordshire*, appeared in 1963 and the forty-sixth and final one in 1974, when Pevsner was 72.

It's not unreasonable then that when it came to 'The Buildings of Wales' Pevsner took a back seat, as Advisory Editor, and handed over the editorial reins to Richard Haslam. Haslam's first volume, published, again by Penguin, in 1979, was *Powys*. The County of Powys, though named after an ancient Welsh kingdom, had at that time existed as a Local Authority for only five years, a product of the 1974 re-organisation of local government. Haslam reflects this fact by breaking down his *Powys* volume into three sections: one for each of the former shire counties of Brecon/Brecknock, Radnor, and Montgomery.

Hay falls in the Brecknock section and its entry begins in the traditional Pevsner way, with a description of St Mary's church. But Hay was in the far north-eastern corner of Brecknock: as soon as you cross the Wye Bridge you are in Radnorshire, and the other side of Cusop Dingle is Herefordshire; so a thorough perambulation (Pevsner's term) of the district, requires two books and a certain amount of page turning.

Richard Haslam's Hay – clockwise from bottom left

"the Regency-fronted UNITED REFORM CHURCH"

"TRINITY METHODIST CHAPEL, with a nice Italianate tower"

"CASTLE… Norman are the S windows to the two floors, the upper one with two round-headed lights and a mullion"

"The BUTTER MARKET,… It is quaintly ambitious, for all its diminutive size – an uncouth Doric temple three bays by nine, and till recently open along seven of those"

"ST MARY. A church appropriated to Brecon Priory and dedicated between 1115 and 1135 collapsed c.1700, leaving only the embattled C15 W tower. The present sub-Georgian nave and short chancel are by Edward Haycock Senior, 1834; big lancets alternating buttresses, and inside, a gallery added round the W and N sides"

Hay: Town of Bookshops

Houses in Oxford Road

'Fresh eggs! Fresh eggs!' Aggie's raucous voice increased in volume. She hobbled round the clock and back again. 'Fresh eggs! Fresh eggs!'

On the Black Hill Chapter XV

The Other Twin Towers

If you travel often between Hay and Knighton, it won't take you long to notice that the towns have many similarities. They are of about the same size, both are in Wales but hard against the English border, both have been agricultural market towns, both have had castles and both cluster around a Victorian clock tower.

Nothing unusual around here about having a clock tower. Richard Haslam describes clock towers as "that indispensable, if now unfashionable, focus of the Mid-Wales towns." Machynlleth has a very impressive one which was built to mark the twenty-first birthday of a local toff (Hey son, you'll never guess what I've got you for your birthday!), Newtown has one on top of a bank, marking Queen Victoria's jubilee, Aberystwyth has a relatively modest little number in a side street and Rhayader, which seems to have come late to the fashion, has a tower built in 1924 to commemorate the dead of the Great War.

But back to Hay and Knighton. Have a look at the pictures. Is it just me, or are these two towers suspiciously similar? Hay's clock tower, Richard Haslam tells us, was built in 1881, but he offers no further detail. Knighton's tower I know, because it says so on the side, was designed by a Hereford architect, and built in 1872. So Knighton got there first. But how long, I have often wondered, did it take anyone to notice?

Love birds: a pair of doves nest above the clock in Hay

Twin towers: Hay, right, and Knighton, left

Hay Castle

The original Hay Castle was 'certainly', says Richard Haslam, built at Swan Bank, close by St Mary's church, in about 1100 AD. To judge by the size of the motte (mound) still visible next to the stock market it must have been a fairly modest affair. According to a plaque placed at the site by the Warren Conservation Committee this early castle was the work of Bernard Newmarch also known as Bernard de Newmarche, a Norman invader who was consolidating his gains after defeating Welsh Brycheiniog.

The present castle is also Norman in origin and indeed still has some Norman window openings, but it is believed to date from about 1200. It was built by Matilda de Breos, says Haslam, or Maud de Valerie, say Wynford Vaughan Thomas and Alun Llewelyn. The latter authors report that Maud, or Matilda, was wife of William de Braose, and has passed into local legend as Maud Walbee. Or Moll Walabee, says Alfred Watkins. Watkins relates that Matilda/Maud/Moll is supposed to have built Hay Castle with her bare hands in just one night, carrying the stones in her apron; but when a big stone got in her shoe she threw it across the river in a temper, and it became a cross in Llowes churchyard. Not a lady to be trifled with.

There was certainly a lot going on in and around Hay Castle in the thirteenth century. Llewelyn ap Iorwerth burned the town in 1231, Henry III had the castle re-built in 1233 and Simon de Montfort had it 'reduced' in 1256.

Red Valerian on the walls of Hay Castle

Hay Castle, with its Norman windows

Saturday, 18th June [1870]

It was very hot walking, a sultry heat. At Hay Castle I found a number of young ladies playing croquet with Pope, Margaret Oswald, Jenny Dew, Lucy Allen, Charlotte and Edith Thomas. At lawn tea Charlotte Thomas emptied her cup of tea into her lap and then in getting up shot part of the contents of her lap out on to Mrs. Allen's dress.

Kilvert's Diary

Attached to the thirteenth century Hay Castle is a seventeenth century mansion, part of which is also currently derelict. The two buildings seem to have grown together over the years, so that until I read Haslam I had not really appreciated that they were not one and the same. Viewed from below, on Castle Street, the combined effect is almost, (but not quite) one of picturesque decay. From the lawns to the rear the mansion certainly looks quite grand, but warning signs and temporary fencing keep the incautious away from the crumbling eastern end. Not for long though, if the Hay Castle Trust has its way.

Formed in 2011 the Trust seeks to restore the castle "as a major centre for culture, arts and education". A high-powered bunch, the Directors include Peter Florence, the Director of the Hay Festival, and Justin Albert, the National Trust's Director for Wales. They want to hear from you: www.haycastletrust.org.uk

The mansion from the south

Overleaf: Hay Castle and Mansion, from Boatside

31

Almost, but not quite, picturesque: the derelict seventeenth century mansion attached to Hay castle

Hay People – Alan Powell, Carpenter

If you have spent much time in Hay you will have noticed Alan Powell's shop front in Broad Street. And you would not be alone, Googling Alan's name I found a photo similar to my own, taken by Alexandra Bone of Norfolk (www.alexandrabone.co.uk). She says:

> Was taken with this building on a recent trip to Hay-on-Wye. Loved the textures of the weathered wood.

I like it too, it has a good, honest, agricultural, Old Hay look about it. Alan is not strictly Hay though, he's from off. Llanfihangel Tal-y-llyn, near Brecon. He learned his trade in Brecon and set up his own business in Hay when he married a local girl in 1969. For 32 of his 44 Hay years Alan was a volunteer fireman too, and Officer in Charge at Hay Fire Station for the last six of these. Now he is a Town Councillor. Alan says he needs to be doing, so, though 'well over 60', he is reluctant to retire. He does take time off though, and, like Johnny Golesworthy, is a keen fisherman. He ties his own flies and fishes in the sea, as well as on the Wye for trout.

A proper old-fashioned tradesman, Alan builds, among other things, traditional sash windows, shop fronts, staircases and Welsh Dressers. I like a good sash window myself, so was pleased to find a stack of used sash weights in his workshop, gathering sawdust while they wait for the right job to come along.

A favourite book? *Indian Cooking* by Madhur Jaffrey. Alan has 300 cookery books. (You weren't expecting that were you!)

An Excursion to the Black Mountains

Head south from Hay, whether it be on the Offa's Dyke Path or by road, and there is no avoiding the Black Mountains. If you take the Path you will before long find yourself climbing the flank of Hay Bluff, with dramatic views over Herefordshire and the Wye Valley. By road you'll be able to take a slightly, but only slightly, lower route, winding up the Welsh side of the mountain to the 538 metre (1,765 foot) Gospel Pass. It's not for nervous drivers. From here you descend, still on a narrow undulating road with passing places, to Capel-y-ffin, in the Vale of Ewyas, with mountains on all sides.

This is hard, high, hill farming country, vividly described in Bruce Chatwin's *On the Black Hill*. The original of his fictional farm The Vision is in this valley, just beyond Capel-y-ffin. Another famous visitor was the sculptor Eric Gill, who lived here in the 1920s. He didn't last though, and neither did the Augustinian monks of Llanthony Priory, a picturesque ruin which has been quietly crumbling away for centuries in this romantic but unforgiving setting. More about Gill and Capel-y-ffin shortly but first we'll carry on down to Llanthony, which is well worth a visit. There are two pubs there to give encouragement, if that helps.

In the Black Mountains

And now it was, that by Papal Authority the Church of St. Mary at Gloucester was confirm'd as a Cell to that of St. John Baptist at Lanthony. However the Canons being better pleased with their new Habitation, which was much braver and richer than their old Seat in Wales, chose to inhabit at Gloucester, removing and spoiling what they had at Lanthony. They became also very licentious in their way of living. During this William their Prior fallng into Troubles and Vexation as well with the Canons of his own House, as Roger Earl of Hereford the Patron, was forced to resign his Office to whom succeeded Clement the Sub-prior.

Sir William Dugdale, *Monasticon Anglicanum*, 1693

Arthur Clark in *The Story of Monmouthshire* reports that Llanthony Priory was founded in the year 1103 by Walter de Lacy, Lord of Ewias. Almost immediately it ran into difficulties and in 1136 a new, less challenging, site was found at Gloucester. Here the monastery of Llanthony Secunda was established. Llanthony Secunda was far more successful and, Clark reports, when Henry VIII dissolved the monasteries it was valued at £748, compared to the deserted Llanthony Prima which was worth only £90.

Both monasteries are now in ruins but their settings are very different. Llanthony Prima, in its mountainous rural idyll (captured by J.M.W. Turner), could hardly be more picturesque. Llanthony Secunda, sadly, could hardly be less so. It is now swallowed up in the flat urban fringe of the city of Gloucester, hemmed in by commercial and industrial development. Just next door is the Llanthony Business Park and across the road Bikini Bathrooms. Such remains as there are of the original buildings are barely recognisable, and you can easily pass them on the A430 without noticing.

Crumbling for centuries: Llanthony Priory

Descending the Gospel Pass

Llanthony Priory, in ruins

The Priory, in the Vale of Ewyas

Romantic: Llanthony Prima

Practical: Llanthony Secunda

Retrace your steps toward Hay for the next chapter (is that a pun? I'm not sure) in the monastic history of hereabouts. In 1869-70 the Rev Joseph Lyne, taking the name Father Ignatius, founded a new monastery at Capel-y-ffin, which is just three miles above Llanthony Prima. He called it Llanthony Tertia. Lyne crops up in both Kilvert's *Diary* and *On the Black Hill*. Kilvert met and conversed with him, Chatwin lightly disguises him, as he did Hay, this time by calling Lyne 'Father Ambrosius'. The Woolhope Naturalists' Field Club, visiting in 1930, refer to a reported appearance of The Virgin at Capel-y-ffin some 47 years before, and Chatwin picks this up as well, giving it as the reason for the naming of The Vision farm.

Joseph Lyne died in 1908 but in 1924 Eric Gill took on his monastery. Gill is famous for, among other things, the controversial sculpture of Prospero and Ariel (that is a pun) on the BBC's Broadcasting House in London. You probably have his typefaces Gill Sans and Perpetua on your computer too. Gill stayed only four years at Capel-y-ffin, yet in his 1940 autobiography he eulogises the simple life among the mountains while railing against the horrors of the modern age to which he so quickly returned.

The monastery buildings of Llanthony Tertia are still there, though not open to the public, and there is a memorial to Lyne/Father Ignatius at the roadside just below them.

The wayside memorial to Father Ignatius

The ruins of the monastery church at Llanthony Tertia

It is interesting to contrast Gill's gloomy prognosis for life in the Black Mountains with Joyce Gervis's happy memories of her childhood fifty years later (see Hay People).

> And we bathed naked all together in the mountain pools and under the waterfalls. And we had heavenly picnics by the Nant-y-buch in little sunny secluded paradises, or climbed the green mountains and smelt the smell of a world untouched by men of business. But alas! that is saying too much, for the evil hand, the outstretched claw of the dealer and financier was bringing ruin all around. The valley, the lovely vale of Ewyas, was never afflicted with his evil presence – his petrol pumps and road-houses, his factory filth and his suburban vulgarity. But his evil influence was over all. The population of the valley was but a quarter of what it had been fifty years before. There were twenty ruined cottages between Capel-y-ffin and Llanthony four miles lower down the valley. The young men had gone to the mines and were wandering unemployed in the Rhondda, their fathers could not call them home for the city of London found it more profitable to foster Australian Capitalist sheep farming than to preserve the thousand-year traditions of the South Wales mountains. We were living in a dying land – unspoiled but dying. It is still the same paradise and it is possible that it will long remain so. For by the mercy of geographical accident all the valleys are cul-de-sacs. Let the industrial-capitalist disease do its worst – the Black Mountains of Brecon will remain untouched and their green valleys lead nowhere.

Afon Honddu

Not dead yet: Llanthony Prima and the Vale of Ewyas

RHULEN – "*1½ miles SE of Cregrina*"

ST DAVID – "*The most unassuming of all the Radnorshire rural churches. White-painted and shaped like a hull – the walls lean out every which way.*"

Richard Haslam

On the Black Hill

Bruce Chatwin's novel *On the Black Hill* was first published, to critical acclaim, in 1982. The cover of my 1983 paperback copy is laden with lavish praise from such literary heavyweights as Auberon Waugh, V.S. Pritchett and John Updike: Chatwin is compared to D.H. Lawrence, Thomas Hardy and Ernest Hemingway.

It's a good book then. And it's a good book about life in the hills around Hay, though the town itself is disguised under the name of Rhulen, which happens to be a tiny village deep in the Radnorshire hills eleven miles to the north west. (The real Rhulen also appears in Kilvert's *Diary*.)

Late on a winter's afternoon I stopped at the roadside to photograph the Black Hill looming against a still bright sky. To my annoyance a farmer on a quad bike suddenly appeared right in the middle of my carefully composed scene. I paused to let him pass, but as he drove across the field in front of me, his dog racing dementedly round and round him, I realised that the two of them just made the picture. Serendipity.

The Black Hill, Craswell

The Vision was an outlying farm on the Lurkenhope Estate... The roofs of the buildings were yellow with stonecrop...

On the Black Hill, Chapter V

Mary slipped on a pair of galoshes and squelched her way across the boggy pasture. The wind moved over the field. The grassheads flashed like shoals of minnows, and there were purple orchids and heads of red sorrel.

On the Black Hill, Chapter XVI

Chatwin's novel is the story of twin brothers Benjamin and Lewis Jones, and of their parents (played by Gemma Jones and Bob Peck in a 1987 film adaptation). The twins spend their entire lives on the family farm, The Vision, neither of them marrying. The book is packed with local references though actual people and places are often lightly disguised. So the Radnorshire Hills, Hereford, and the England-Wales border feature, as does a farm called Cockalofty, which in real life is just below Hay Bluff. The real Vision farm is in the Vale of Ewyas, close to Capel y ffin, and the Black Hill of the title, also known as the Cat's Back, is just across the border in the Herefordshire parish of Craswall. The sundial of Maesyronnen Chapel gets a mention, along with the Rev Joseph Lyne.

More importantly Chatwin's book, it is widely agreed, captures the essence of the hard life of the hill farming community in the Welsh borders. Local girl Joyce Gervis certainly thinks so, and she knows better than most.

An English translation of Capel-y-ffin is "the border, or boundary, chapel", and there are two chapels there. At the roadside stands the tiny Church of St Mary described by Kilvert as "short, stout and boxy", while on the far side of the infant Afon Honddu is a less well known Baptist chapel, built in 1737. The headstones in the cemetery here offer some fascinating reading.

CRASWALL

"ST MARY. Nave and chancel and bell-turret. The W part of the church is used as a lobby and vestry. It was cut off by a wall in the C18. Original Perp chancel windows with ogee-headed lights and straighttops. The chancel roof has in the E bays some foliage decoration of the purlins."

Nikolaus Pevsner

Shortly after taking my picture of the Black Hill, I came across the exquisite little parish church of St Mary, Craswall, which I had seen just once, at least twenty years before, and had never been able to find again. Utterly unspoiled, unmodernised and little-visited, it is barely visible on the Ordnance Survey map. Even the sign at the roadside, faded and weather beaten, seems reluctant to draw attention to itself, but the church is well worth seeking out. I'll let you find it for yourself so that you can experience the joy of discovery as I did.

On the gate to the porch at St Mary's I found a memorial plaque to a real Lewis (or Benjamin) Jones: William Watkins of Dukes Farm, who lived eighty-eight years in the parish and died in 1994, five years after Chatwin.

St Mary's church, Craswall

...beyond rose the Radnor hills, their humped outlines receding grey on grey towards the end of the world.

On the Black Hill Chap X

Hay People – Joyce Gervis, Businesswoman

Joyce Gervis's family has farmed the Black Mountains for generations. She grew up literally in the shadow of Hay Bluff, on its sun-starved north-western flank, just below the Gospel Pass. Her grandparents had the Chapel Farm over the pass at Capel y ffin, and her own parents were married at St Mary's Craswall, so Joyce is steeped in the landscape and culture of these parts.

Nevertheless she left the farm at sixeen, first to move to Hay and later, like so many youngsters from rural Wales, to an even bigger place. Hackney, in fact. Joyce wasn't there long though, and came back to Llangorse, near Brecon, where she and her husband Nigel bought Tŷ-Mawr (the Big House), on the shores of Llangorse Lake.

Needing materials to restore Tŷ-Mawr, Joyce and Nigel set about researching traditional lime-based building techniques. Now they have their own company, Tŷ-Mawr Lime, and supply environmentally-friendly paints, plasters and mortars to, among others, the Prince of Wales. Their products include 'Glaster', a lime plaster which uses recycled glass in place of the conventional sand or vermiculite. Tiny pieces of coloured glass make the unpainted material sparkle. Pretty, but damned difficult to photograph.

Tŷ-Mawr and Llangorse lake

Joyce and a customer

By a display Glaister panel

Joyce loved growing up on a farm:

> My father was passionate about horses when we lived on the mountain and so we spent our young lives on horseback. It was the best way to get around the farm with all those hills! My other grandparents farmed above Velindre so we would ride over there too – to get eggs if we had run out – it was fantastic! As we had land adjoining the hill, we had rights to graze the mountains. We would gather our horses from the hill (on horseback) twice a year to bring the foals in to wean from their mothers and then to sell. We had Welsh Mountain ponies who survived well out there and then cobs mostly, to ride. Beautiful animals. Mum worked on the farm always. From age 6 she kept chickens and turkeys. Quite a hard life, and now at 72 she still farms. She loves her cattle and sheep. Until 2010, when my father died, she was still showing them and winning prizes. She won the Welsh flock competition for a couple of years, she's a great farmer.

A favourite book? "*On the Black Hill*, of course."

Grazing Hay Bluff, 2012

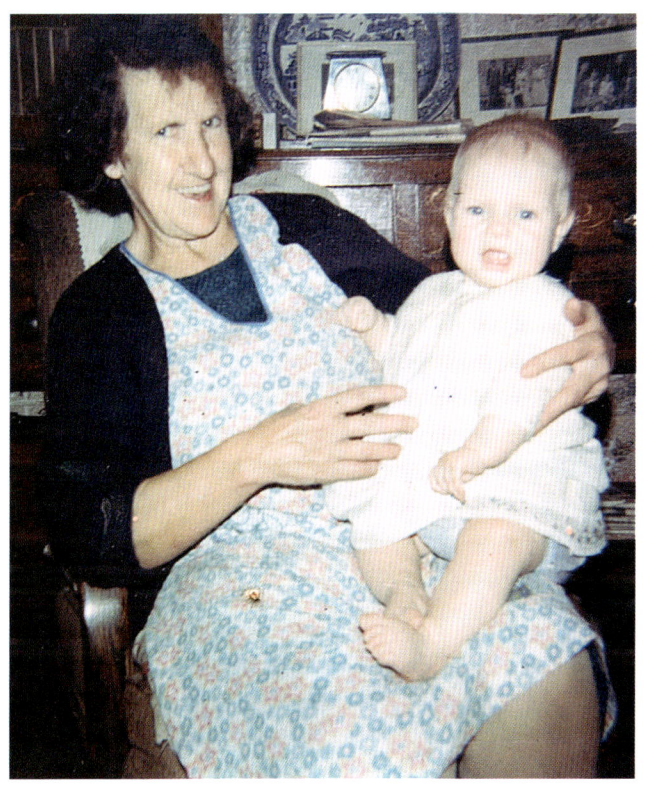

From Joyce Gervis' family album

bottom: Dad, with one of his beloved horses

Mum, also with horses!

Joyce with her grandmother, Gwen Morgan, at Chapel Farm, Capel-y-ffin

The Hay Festival

In 2012 the Hay Festival, full title The Hay Festival of Literature and the Arts, celebrated its 25th anniversary, and in those 25 years it has grown and grown. It is now not only one of the UK's most prestigious arts events but also a worldwide brand. Writers from around the globe come to the Hay Festival and the Hay Festival returns the favour. Visit www.hayfestival.com and you will see that there are now Hay Festivals in Mexico, Canada, Peru, Spain, Turkey, Lebanon – fourteen locations in all, in twelve countries. I was a little surprised recently to receive a press report about the Hay Festival from the *Daily Star*. Now the *Daily Star* that I see in my local newsagent is, how shall I put it, not a particularly literary publication. It turned out this was the Dhaka *Daily Star*, reporting on Bangladesh's second Hay Festival.

When Norman and Rhoda Florence started the Festival in 1987 the town was already well established as a literary destination, famous for its second-hand bookshops. This first literary incarnation had been led by Richard Booth, who ran bookshops himself, lived in Hay Castle and styled himself King of Hay. There was a certain amount of friction in the early days: I recall a T-shirt sold in Booth's shops which characterised the Hay Festival as being for 'Arts, Tarts and Farts'. And I was in the room when Peter Florence, who had taken on the festival from his parents, exclaimed on first seeing Richard Booth queueing for a Hay Festival event.

It's always sunny at the Hay Festival

I worked at the Festival in the 1990s, when it took place in Hay's Primary School during half-term week, and we drivers were volunteers, doing it just for fun. And it was fun. But even back then the festival was a hugely complicated event. Sometimes things went wrong, as when one of the drivers disappeared off the map with a big name writer and it was realised that, not only did no-one know where they had gone, but no-one knew anything about the driver. I joked that perhaps he was an axe-murderer, which went down well. Occasionally when the admin staff were all busy I would pick up the office phone, which is how I got involved in trying to track down a famous author on behalf of the Prince of Wales, who wanted to meet him.

Now Hay has outgrown both the school and half-term week, and it has moved to its own dedicated site on the edge of the town. Of course this gives the organisers much more flexibilty, but it has not solved all their difficulties. The 2012 Festival was a wet one and many of the car parks, on local farmers fields, soon became waterlogged. When they were closed punters started to park on roadsides, and I had to resort to local knowledge and my Ordnance Survey map to get Andrew Marr to his event through rural traffic chaos.

"So, Jim, who else did you have in your car?" I hear you ask.

I collected legendary travel writer Norman Lewis and his wife from their home in Essex and brought them to Hay. Quiet, unpretentious people, they were happy to have lunch at a Little Chef. Similarly I brought Sue Townsend from home in Leicester to Hay and later took her back. Lovely lady, sadly missed. I took Melvyn Bragg from Hay

It's always *sunny at the* Hay Festival

Getting down to some serious reading

Hay babes Annabel Andrews and friend, 2009

Literature is big in Hay

to Newport station. We were in a bit of a hurry to catch his train and, as he had just done an event with Richard Dawkins and John Maddox, we ended up discussing the Darwinian implications of overtaking slow traffic. I collected Helen Fielding from Newport. She had a hangover and a friend who I later realised was restaurant critic of the *Independent*. At the Festival everyone called Helen 'Bridget', and when she got confused signing a book for me I could see why.

I took someone called Graham Swift to Newport and next thing I knew he was on the *Today* programme, having won the Booker prize. The following year I was sent to pick up an author with a foreign name from Hereford Station. A petite young Indian woman, she too went on to win the Booker. It was Arundhati Roy. I was tasked with entertaining her husband, who was interested in forestry and could not believe the narrow country lanes around Hay. He made me stop so that he could take a photo of the car brushing the hedges on both sides.

In 2013 I was sent to collect Colm Toibin from his accommodation in Hay and bring him to site, but he decided to walk instead. He was shortlisted for the Booker that year but, strangely, failed to win…

The late lamented Stephen Jay Gould, an anglophile American who had once lived in Oxford, was very keen on church architecture. In the drive back from Heathrow airport we paused to admire churches in Cirencester, Dymock and Birdlip (all in Gloucestershire) and finally at Hereford Cathedral, where he insisted on taking me to see the Mappa Mundi.

There was Tina Brown (then editor of *The New Yorker*) and husband Harold Evans, Ismail Merchant (of Merchant-Ivory films), who bought me an ice-cream, Hanif Kureishi & entourage, David Jenkins the controversial former Bishop of Durham, up at crack of dawn and waiting outside for me when I arrived. I wasn't there for Bill Clinton but I did get a Press Pass to photograph Al Gore, (and do you know, not long after that he won the Nobel Peace Prize!).

In 2012 Alistair Darling, former Chancellor of the Exchequer, gave me the lowdown on Scottish political skullduggery and was very interested in the Range Rover's intelligent cruise control, which keeps the car going at a steady speed, up hill and down dale. Was he thinking metaphorically? TV historian Bettany Hughes was not in my car but helped me out of a scrape by giving me telephone directions to the remote house where she was staying. Andrew Marr probably wished he was not in my car either (see above *re* traffic chaos). Ian Rankin, who had not been to Hay for many years, was under the impression that it was still a fairly sleepy agricultural town. Well, I suppose compared to Edinburgh... Ian McEwan, who lives very close to the farm where my grandmother grew up. Terry Pratchett, who was on his way to a photo shoot with some pigs. Sarah Crompton, Arts Editor of the *Daily Telegraph* who seemed a very nice lady and who I recognised soon after on television in *Newsnight Review*.

I had the opportunity to take Salman Rushdie and Alan Yentob to London, but I'm not keen on driving in the big city so I ducked out of that one. Nothing to do with the Fatwa. In the office kitchen I met Tom Watson MP, scourge of the Murdoch empire. He's a personal hero of mine so I insisted on shaking his hand. Probably not supposed to do that.

It's all about the books

A typical array of talent at the Festival

Hay: Town of Books
– and readers

Hay People – Max Pfefferkorn

Each Spring thousands of people walk along the Brecon Road, between the Festival site and Hay town centre. They pass, probably not noticing, the municipal cemetery, in one corner of which is a neatly mown patch of grass containing just seventeen war graves. British, Italian and German soldiers lie side by side. Among them is Max Pfefferkorn.

Max Pfefferkorn was born on 5th April 1903, so he was not a young soldier in World War II. But whereas most of his compatriots commemorated here died in 1945 or 1946, in a prisoner of war camp in Brecon, Pfefferkorn lived three years beyond the war to die, still in Wales, in January 1948. I wonder why this might be? Was he too ill to return home after the war, or did he have no home to return to?

Initially it appeared to me that the latter was the case. The German memorial website www.weltkriegsopfer.de records Pfefferkorn as having been born in Arnswalde, a small town in Pomerania, a much-disputed region on the border between Germany and Poland. Early in 1945 Pomerania was overrun by the Soviet Army and after the war Arnswalde, now Choszczno, became part of Poland. Germans there were expelled.

However at the 2013 Hay Festival I collected author and *Guardian* journalist Ian Cobain from Hereford Station, who offered an alternative narrative. He told me that after World War II many prisoners-of-war were kept in the U.K. until 1947 or 1948 to work as farm labour. Eventually the British government came under pressure from the Americans, who were trying to persuade Stalin to return his German prisoners and felt that Britain was not helping the cause. Rather than simply being sent back en masse the Germans were classified according to their background. 'Good' Germans returned first, members of the Nazi party or Waffen SS were detained for longer.

Perhaps Max Pfefferkorn would eventually have returned to part of post-war Germany, or have settled, as some former prisoners of war did, in the U.K. But it was not to be, and he lies in Hay, between L Sjt 7578156 T.C. Macdonald of the Royal Army Ordnance Corps and Soldier Lisiade Giroldi, of the Esercito Italiano.

The oldest surviving chapel in Wales, Maesyronnen, near Hay-on-Wye was converted from a cow-house in 1696, and is still largely in original condition.

Anthony Jones *Welsh Chapels*

The Chapel at Maesyfelin was one of the oldest Non-Conformist chapels in the country. A long stone building, devoid of decoration but for a sundial over the door, it lay between the stream and the lane, encircled by a windbreak of Portuguese laurel.

On the Black Hill Chapter XVII

Chapel

Hay may be only just in Wales, but in Wales it is, and therefore we must talk about chapel. And where better to start than the oldest chapel in Wales, Maesyronnen, which is just three miles west of Hay, near Glasbury. I say 'near Glasbury' because this chapel is pretty much in the middle of nowhere, standing on its own, surrounded by fields, as it has done for more than 300 years. And there is a reason for this, just as there is a reason why it is a very plain, undecorated building.

For the greater part of the seventeenth century Nonconformist Christians, those who refused to conform to the rules of the Established (Anglican) Church, were a persecuted minority in England and Wales. Fearful of discovery, they met in secret, in out-of-the-way places and in whatever buildings were available. In the case of Maesyronnen this appears, in the beginning, to have been a cowshed. The six-page booklet provided for visitors makes fascinating reading. The Conventicle Act of 1664, it tells us, made it illegal for more than five people to gather for a religious meeting anywhere other than as part of the Anglican church. And in case this did not offer sufficient discouragement to 'dissenters' the Five Mile Act, a year later, forbade a Nonconformist minister to come within five miles of any town, or to teach in a public school.

Maesyronnen Chapel, the oldest in Wales

But even when dissent became respectable life remained hard for the congregation of Maesyronnen. There is a memorial in the chapel to Mary Lloyd, wife of the Reverend Richard Lloyd, who died in 1840 aged 38, having born and lost no fewer than three children. Even so she is commemorated with the bible quotation "Thanks be unto God for his unspeakable gift". Another tablet lists the one daughter and two sons of John and Mary Prosser, who died between 1825 and 1844, aged 7, 29 and 40.

In his book *Welsh Chapels*, published in 1996, Anthony Jones traces the development both of Nonconformism and of chapel architecture in Wales. He emphasises that, in the early days at least, a chapel was not a building but a group of people. Their building was just a place to gather, and was therefore often very plain and functional. But over time both the chapel members and the chapel buildings became more ambitious. Chapels proliferated and they grew bigger, grander, and much more expensive, with congregations often getting into debt to pay for them.

Just over a mile south of Maesyronnen, Treble Hill Baptist Chapel, across the Wye Bridge from Glasbury, has some features typical of later urban chapels. Its gable end faces the road, enabling it to fit into a narrow plot of land, with other buildings on either side. Its street facade is of red brick, rather than the local stone of Maesyronnen, and is in the Classical style. So it is perfectly symmetrical and has closely-jointed stone

Mary Lloyd's memorial, Maesyronnen

Classical: Treble Hill Baptist Chapel

pilasters, which imitate classical columns, and give the impression of supporting the triangular pediment, which in turn conceals the roof. Treble Hill was built in 1866.

Back in Hay the Bethesda Evangelical Church, in Oxford Road, was built the year before Treble Hill Baptist. It is also faced with red brick, but this time is in the rival neo-Gothic style. So no fake columns, a pointed arch over the door and just a little stone window tracery, in the Decorated style. Bethesda was originally a Primitive Methodist Chapel and when I photographed it in 2008 carried these words in beautifully carved stone across its frontage. I was shocked, when I returned to photograph the church again in 2012, to find that they had disappeared. Not quite Gothic horror but certainly Gothic disappointment.

Just around the corner from Bethesda Evangelical, in Hay's Bull Ring, is the Salem Baptist Chapel, which, like Maesyronnen, dates back to the very early days of Nonconformism. A board by the chapel door tells us that it was founded in 1649, though the present building dates from 1878.

Gothic: Bethesda Primitive Methodist Chapel

Salem Baptist Chapel

IN LOVING MEMORY
OF
ELIJA WATKINS
WHO DIED JAN. 2ND 1858.
AGED 49 YEARS.

ALSO OF LUCY DAUGHTER OF
ELIJA AND PHEBE WATKINS
BORN 11TH JUNE
DIED 31ST OCT

"BLESSED ARE THE DEAD

Hay People – Kirsty Williams, A.M.

I first met Kirsty Williams when she turned up on my doorstep one day, canvassing to become a candidate in the first ever elections for the Welsh Assembly. She clearly knew what she was doing and I concluded that she would go far. Sure enough in 1999 Kirsty was duly elected the first Assembly Member (AM) for Hay, which is in the constituency of Brecon and Radnorshire. She has been there ever since and is now leader of the Liberal Democrats in the Assembly.

Kirsty is part of a great Mid-Wales tradition of non-conformity (see 'Chapel') and independent thought. The MP for Brecon and Radnor, Roger Williams, is also a Liberal Democrat, as was, for many years, the Member for neighbouring Montgomeryshire. The two major Westminster parties have never held much sway around here, and many local politicians are either Liberal or Independent. The Local Authority for Hay, Powys County Council, has a majority of independent members, not affiliated to any political party.

It helps to have local roots too. Roger Williams has a farm near Brecon, as do Kirsty and her husband. Kirsty is no yokel though, she has studied at the Universities of Manchester and Missouri.

Kirsty hates having her photograph taken which, I pointed out to her, is a bit of a handicap for one in her line of work. It doesn't seem to have done her any harm though.

Her favourite book is *Native Son* by Richard Wright, America's best-selling black writer. It was first published in 1940.

Kirsty Williams in the sybaritic surroundings of her constituency surgery in Knighton

Saturday, 5 March [1870]

Very cold last night, and sharp frost and the day brilliant and the air exquisitely clear though the wind was East. The view from the banks lovely, the river winding down from Glasbury like a silver serpent, flowing beneath at the foot of the poplars. Hay in the distance bright in brilliant sunshine.

Kilvert's Diary

Kilvert and Clyro

One cannot travel far around Hay without coming across the name Kilvert, for the town is slap in the middle of 'Kilvert Country', made famous by the Rev Francis Kilvert and his diary of a Victorian country curate.

The published extracts of *Kilvert's Diary* cover the period 1870 to 1879, during which he rose from being a humble curate at Clyro to become, in 1877, rector of the Herefordshire parish of Bredwardine. Clyro is just a mile across the valley from Hay, while Bredwardine is eight miles east, on the back road to Hereford. Furthermore Kilvert's sister was married to the Vicar of Monnington-on-Wye, which is just beyond Bredwardine. All of these are archetypal village communities set in real countryside, picturesquely described by Kilvert and remaining picturesque to this day. It's a marketing man's dream.

The young Kilvert spent a good deal of his time tramping this countryside, visiting outlying farms and cottages, but he also paid regular visits to Hay, and to Hay Castle in particular, where he always hoped to see Daisy Thomas, another a regular visitor, with whom he was enraptured. But it was not to be:

Saturday, 23 September [1871]

A letter came from Mr. Thomas. Kindly expressed and cordial, but bidding me give up all thoughts and hopes of Daisy. It was a great and sudden blow and I felt very sad. The sun seemed to have gone out of the sky.

Kilvert's church at Clyro: St. Michael's

> It is difficult for me to conceive of any more agreeable way of life than that of the Victorian country parson. If I had to choose my ideal span of life I should choose to have been born in the 1830s, the son of a parson with the genetic inheritance of strong teeth.
>
> A.N. Wilson, *The Victorians*

Although Kilvert's fascination with young girls has an unfortunate contemporary resonance we are left in no doubt that he was a sensitive soul, and one well suited to a quiet country life:

> Monday, 6 March [1871] I like wandering about these lonely, waste and ruined places. There dwells among them a spirit of quiet and gentle melancholy more congenial and akin to my own spirit than full life and gaiety and noise.

But he does seem to have had a sense of humour too:

> Wednesday, 9 February [1870] Hannah Jones smoking a short black pipe by the fire, and her daughter, a young mother with dark eyes and her hair hanging loose, nursing her baby and displaying her charms liberally.

William Plomer, of publishers Jonathan Cape, introduced the diary to a wider world in 1938. Initially it was published in three parts, in succeeding years, so that the third appeared in 1940, a year when one can imagine it might have been particularly in tune with patriotic sentiment in beleaguered Britain. Plomer, who had edited the diaries, also provided an Introduction, which reveals that the three notebooks to which he had access were but a fraction of the original collection, at least nineteen others having been destroyed by members of the Kilvert family.

Kilvert records many tragedies, both local and national, in his diary, including at least three suicides, and Plomer's introduction suggests that the diarist's own life ended with a cruel twist. Although he was a keen student of feminine beauty Kilvert was 39 before he finally married; only to die just one month later. He had no children and his wife did not remarry.

Kilvert memorial at Bredwardine church

The Wye at Bredwardine Bridge

Monday 28 November 1870

Walked up the Cwm and found old James Jones stonebreaking. He told me now he was once travelling from Hereford to Hay by coach when the coach was wrecked in a flood by Bredwardine Bridge because the coachman would not take the bearing reins of the horses off. The bearing reins kept the noses of the horses down under water. They plunged and reared and got the coach off the road and swimming like a boat, and an old lady inside screaming horribly.

Kilvert's Diary

Tuesday 30th August 1870

Hay Flower Show, the first they have had, a very successful one. A nice large tent, the poles prettily wreathed with hop vine, and the flowers fruit and vegetables prettily arranged. There was an excursion train from Builth to Hay for the occasion. The town was hung with flags. The whole country was there.

Kilvert's Diary

However, in a memorial service conducted at St Michael's church Clyro on 7th July 1946, the Bishop of Swansea and Brecon cast further light on the later years of Kilvert's life. It seems that his health had been poor for some time before he married and that he was aware that he might not reach a ripe old age. So it may well be that he and his new wife knew well enough what was in store, even on their wedding day.

John Phillips, who was Transport Manager, and therefore my boss, at the Hay Festival in the 1990's lived at one time in Brobury, a small village just across the Wye from Bredwardine. He was told by villagers that when Kilvert was married his parishioners decorated all the trees which lined his route from Bredwardine church via Brobury to the Hereford Road, so that he passed them en route to his honeymoon. When his coffin returned to the village the following month it took the same route, and the decorations were still there.

A view across the Wye Valley above Hay from Maesyronnen Chapel. According to an anecdote in Kilvert, the poet Wordsworth "used to say that the Wye was the finest piece of scenery in South Britain."

Monday, 8 July [1872]

Reports coming in all day of the mischief done by yesterday's flood. Pigs, sheep, calves swept away from meadow and cot and carried down the river with hundreds of tons of hay, timber, hurdles and, it is said, furniture. The roads swept bare to the very lock. Culverts choked and blown up, turnips washed out of the ground on the hillsides, down into the orchards and turnpike roads. Four inches of mud in the Rhydspence Inn on the Welsh side of the border, the Sun, Lower Cabalva House flooded again and the carpets out to dry. Pastures covered with grit and gravel and rendered useless and dangerous for cattle till after the next heavy rain.

Kilvert's Diary

Septuagesima Sunday, St Valentine's Eve

Preached at Clyro in the morning (Matthew xiv, 30). Very few people in Church, the weather fearful, violent deadly E. wind and the hardest frost we have had yet. Went to Bettws in the afternoon wrapped in two waistcoats, two coats, a muffler and a mackintosh, and was not at all too warm. Heard the Chapel bell pealing strongly for the second time since I have been here and when I got to the Chapel my beard moustaches and whiskers were so stiff with ice that I could hardly open my mouth and my beard was frozen on to my mackintosh. There was a large christening party from Llwyn Gwilym. The baby was baptized in ice which was broken and swimming about in the Font.

Kilvert's Diary

An Excursion to Bettws Clyro

As luck would have it on the day that I went to visit Kilvert's chapel at Bettws Clyro there had been a heavy frost overnight. But times have changed and I only had to remove ice from my car, not my whiskers, as Kilvert did. It was a glorious sunny Sunday morning though, and when I arrived at the chapel a service was in progress.

Not wishing to intrude I made the most of the sunshine and took some pictures outside while I waited for the congregation to emerge. Below the cloudless blue sky red seemed to be the theme. A red Landrover was parked by the chapel gate and a couple of red-breasted Robins were having a noisy dispute in a thorn hedge full of red haws. A solitary red coat hung in the chapel doorway too.

The church of the Holy Trinity at Bettws Clyro does not have many modern advantages. There is no road to it, and therefore no car park, and in this respect it is even more remote than Maesyronnen. It is a good deal harder to find too, standing alone between two fields away to the side of an un-marked track. But, though Kilvert refers to Holy Trinity as a chapel, it is not, like Maesyronnen, a chapel in the Nonconformist sense. This church in a field is Anglican, or Church in Wales as it is called in Wales.

A solitary red coat

A sunny Sunday at Bettws Clyro

HOLY TRINITY *(till 1878)*. *A simple rectangle almost completely rebuilt in 1878-9. The roof however is C14, perhaps. It has two scissor trusses combined with king-post pendants alternating with three arch-braced collar trusses, and two carved figures, holding shields, as corbels over the chancel. – SCREEN. Inserted below the E scissor beam. Two moulded uprights with capitals and spandrel pieces supporting the rood beam survive. There are no signs that there was any tracery. On top has been set the gallery front of twelve simply pierced bays. Dated by Crossley as late C14 or early C15. – FONT. C13; circular and tapering.*

The Buildings of Wales – Powys

The Rev. David Thomas at Bettws Clyro

Roof timbers at Bettws Clyro and, inset, Richard Lister Venables's signature

According to the *Transactions of the Radnorshire Society* (Vol LXXVII, 2007)

> Since the beginning of the eighteenth century (and probably long before) the tiny church of the Holy Trinity at Betws [sic] Clyro has been a chapel of ease attached to Clyro Parish Church...

The Transactions go on to relate how, when the chapel was completely rebuilt in 1878 the old roof timbers were carefully preserved and re-erected in their original configuration. A commendable effort which enables what is, in fact, a Victorian Church to retain a convincingly ancient and rustic ambience.

[A note on nomenclature: In common with many place names close to the English border the spelling of 'Bettws Clyro' seems to vary. My Welsh/English dictionary gives 'betws' as meaning chapel or oratory, but a book review in the *Radnorshire Transactions* of 1932 reports that 'about eleven' meanings have been suggested for the word.]

To return to my sunny Sunday: the service duly ended and I was able to meet the man who had taken the place occupied by Francis Kilvert on Septuagesima Sunday in 1870. He was the Reverend David Thomas, Vicar of the Wye Valley Group of Parishes (which are Glasbury, Llowes, Clyro and Bettws). He told me that the Kilvert Society had paid a visit not long before and had been very excited to discover that the bible at Bettws Clyro still bore the signature, dated January 1st 1865, of Richard Lister Venables, the vicar under whom Kilvert had served as curate. Said bible was duly produced and photographed.

This was starting to look like a good day.

Hay People – David Eckley, Farmer

David Eckley and I met at the 2012 Hay Festival, where we were both drivers. Now Hay drivers are a motley crew from all walks of life but I was nevertheless surprised to learn that David was also a farmer. So here was New Hay and Old Hay under one cap.

Later, when I was looking for someone who worked the land to add to my collection of Hay People David naturally came to mind. I met him at his farm: Lower Cwmgwannon, Clyro, where I quickly discovered that there is more to the man than meets the eye.

David came to Clyro in 1996 from Vowchurch in Herefordshire, where he had grown up on a farm and lived for 54 years. Here, between 1970 and 1996 he bred racehorses: top-flight National Hunt stallions. Sat at the wheel of his Land Rover David reeled off a list of names which included Cruise Missile, Little Wolf and Dering Rose, this last a Cheltenham Festival winner ridden by John Francome. This was interesting, but what really made me sit up was the revelation that David's mother, Gwenda Stokes, grew up at Monnington Court, Vowchurch, which I had recently discovered to be one of the alleged burial places of Owain Glyndŵr. And it turned out that the farm was still in the family, being run by David's cousin Richard Stokes. So David's mother was Herefordshire. His paternal grandfather was too, but Herefordshire hard by Hay: Grandad Eckley farmed at Llydyadyway, Cusop.

When we spoke at Cwmgwannon David was on the point of retiring, and had already bought a house up the valley past Glasbury, but the next generation of his family is still very much involved in agriculture. Son James is high up in the Young Farmers movement, son Jonathan is similarly elevated in the Meat and Livestock Commission and produces market reports for the farming press, and stepson Charlie is a farm manager in Suffolk. Only daughter Kate has entirely escaped the land: she is a solicitor in that London.

Favourite book? *One Hell of a Ride*, the autobiography of champion jockey Paul Carberry.

Finally he decided to consult Mr Arkwright. The solicitor … lived with his ailing wife in a mock-Tudor villa called The Cedars and prided himself on a lawn free of dandelions. There were those who said there was 'something fishy about the fellow'.

A brass plaque, engraved with his name in Roman capitals, gleamed outside his office at Number 14 Broad Street.

On the Black Hill – Chapter XXII

Dandelion Dead

Hay solicitor Herbert Armstrong was hanged in 1922 for the murder of his wife with arsenic; the case was a cause célèbre. Seventy-two years later, the Armstrong case was given fresh publicity, by a television series *Dandelion Dead*, filmed in Hay and prominently featuring the town clock in the title sequence. Michael Kitchen played Armstrong as an amiable incompetent while Sarah Miles's Mrs Armstrong was a horrible harridan. Davies, the pharmacist who supplied Armstrong with the arsenic, supposedly to kill the dandelions in his lawn, was played by Bernard Hepton, and his wife by actress Rhoda Lewis, who in real life is the mother of Hay Festival Director Peter Florence.

In 1995 the story was given a fresh twist. In a new book and an event at the Hay Festival another Hay solicitor, Martin Beales, argued that Armstrong had been a victim of a miscarriage of justice. Beales died of cancer in 2010 and his obituary in *The Daily Telegraph* reveals that *Dandelion Dead* actually facilitated the publication of his book. Armstrong's surviving daughter, it reports, was

> so incensed by the programme's unflattering portrayal of her father that she telephoned Beales the following morning and not only urged him to go ahead with his book, but also gave him access to the entire defence files, which were stored, still intact, in Hereford.

The office where both Beales and Armstrong worked is still there, Williams, Beales & Co. at No 9 Broad Street, Hay, and another event, at Hay 2013, marked the re-publication of Beales's book *Dead Not Buried: Herbert Rowse Armstrong*.

The Wye

The River Wye rises high in the mountains of Mid Wales and passes through the towns of Rhayader and Builth Wells before reaching Hay. Further downstream the city of Hereford is built on the Wye, as are Ross-on-Wye (no, really), Monmouth and Chepstow. It is a beautiful river. Wordsworth is reported by Kilvert to have said that the Wye above Hay was 'the finest piece of scenery in South Britain', and indeed the Lower Wye Valley, from Ross to Chepstow, is officially recognised as an Area of Outstanding Natural Beauty. Wordsworth went there too, and even penned a poem about it 'Lines written a few miles above Tintern Abbey', in which he wrote:

> How oft, in spirit, have I turned to thee, oh sylvan Wye

The whole length of the Wye is also labelled a Site of Special Scientific Interest. Though nicely alliterative this is a term which does not quite conjure up the same romantic image, which is unfortunate, because what it actually means is that this is a river rich in wildlife, one of the most natural and unspoiled in England or Wales. It is particularly famous for salmon.

Go down to the Wye at Hay Festival time and you can expect to find the medicinal herb Comfrey growing along the banks. Don't pick anything you find there though, unless you are really confident with your botany: the deadly poisonous Hemlock Water Dropwort also lines the water's edge. A little later in the season there will be Himalayan Balsam too. This plant is definitely not popular with the Special Scientists: it is an alien invader which has spread widely along Britain's rivers, obliterating all in its path. The exploding seed pods are rather fun though.

The Wye upstream of Hay

Herb farmer Paul Richards, of Hay, cultivates Comfrey on his smallholding in Herefordshire; and nature writer Richard Mabey has a nice quotation about it from *Gerard's Herbal* of 1597:

> The slimie substance of the roote made in a posset of ale, and given to drinke against the paine of the backe, gotten by any violent motion, as wrestling or over much use of women, doth in fower or five daies perfectly cure the same...

If you want to take a closer look at the Wye there are several ways you can do so in the vicinity of Hay. The northbound Offa's Dyke Path follows the west bank of the river downstream from Hay bridge: look for the fingerpost and information board at the far end of the bridge from the town. Alternatively if you walk a little farther up the road from here toward Clyro you will be able to turn left onto the Wye Valley Walk, which will soon bring you back to the bank of the river and then upstream to the village of Llowes.

If the Wye Valley Walk sounds a little too energetic then find your way instead to The Warren, a public open space which is enclosed in a loop of the river west of the town. Here you can sit on a pebbley beach and just watch the Wye go by.

Or perhaps that is all a little dry for you. A number of companies offer canoe hire on the river and some will even set you off to paddle downstream and then pick you up later and bring you back by road. Treat the river with respect though. In summer it may look very inviting for a dip, but it is unpredictable and there have been at least two tragic drownings in recent years.

Poisonous: Hemlock Water Dropwort

Morning-after plant: Comfrey

Crack willows (left) are so called because of their habit of splitting and shedding branches without warning, as their Latin name, 'Salix fragilis', suggests. This is not the willow from which England's cricket bats are made...

'Nice? It's the only thing,' said the Water Rat solemnly, as he leant forward for his stroke. 'Believe me, my young friend, there is nothing – absolutely nothing – half so much worth doing as simply messing about in boats.' (The Wind in the Willows)

Hay People – Johnny Golesworthy, publican

Johnny Golesworthy is landlord of the Blue Boar in Hay, but really he'd rather be fishing. He has fished all his life, game fishing with flies, for trout and salmon. When he was a boy, he says, you could see salmon jumping at the Warren. Now he reckons they are nearly all gone, though trout have improved in recent years following river restoration work by the Wye & Usk Foundation.

Pete Dorling directed me to Johnny in 2008, when I was helping ITV Central to film a series of short pieces about the Offa's Dyke Path. We arranged an interview on the banks of the Wye, where Johnny talked fishing with Central's veteran newscaster Bob Warman. On the opposite bank a beady-eyed heron monitored proceedings and a pair of mute swans watched over their family of six downy cygnets.

Five years later I paid a visit to the Blue Boar to learn little more about Johnny. As it turned out I learned quite a bit about Hay in the process.

Johnny grew up in Hay and met his wife Lucinda at the Primary School, which was then in the centre of town, in Heol y Dwr. There was a mill stream running down Heol y Dwr feeding a mill pond at the bottom of Broad Street, opposite the United Reformed church, which is now The Globe. So this will be where Heol y Dwr gets its name, which means, in English, Water Street. Johnny was always told to keep away from the mill pond.

A rival fisherman looks on (above)

Johnny Golesworthy with Bob Warman on the banks of the Wye

Tuesday 8th March 1870

Yesterday there was an inquest at the Blue Boar, Hay, on the body of the barmaid of the Blue Boar who a day or two ago went out at night on an hour's leave, but went up the Wye to Glasbury and threw herself into the river. She was taken out at Llan Hennw. She was enceinte.

Kilvert's Diary

After Hay Primary Johnny went to Brecon Grammar School, by train for his first eighteen months, until Dr Beeching intervened and the line was closed. The site of Hay's former station is now occupied by the Co-op supermarket, and is in England.

The Golesworthys originally came from Honiton and Ottery St Mary in Devon but Johnny's great-grandfather bought the Granary, by Hay's clock tower, in 1871, and opened the Golesworthy shop, which is now run by Johnny's brother. The rest of the Granary was a grain store for Marstons of Ludlow until about 1970 but the very popular café which now occupies the building is another Golesworthy enterprise, managed by Johnny's sisters. Johnny bought the Blue Boar, which was known to Kilvert, in 1985, and says he has nearly finished paying for it.

When asked for a favourite book Johnny did not hesitate. "*The Cruel Sea* by Nicholas Monserrat, beautiful English"

1920s advertisement for Golesworthy and Sons

Scene of tragedy, the Wye from Glasbury Bridge

An Excursion with Alfred Watkins, Ley Hunter

Depending on your point of view Alfred Watkins either discovered, or invented, ley lines. And it was in the countryside of Herefordshire and the borders, around Hay, that he did it. He knew the area well, having travelled it as a young man selling beer to local pubs for his father's Hereford brewery.

A pillar of the community Watkins was a keen amateur archaeologist, a Fellow of the Royal Photographic Society, inventor of the Watkins exposure meter, a President of the Hereford-based Woolhope Naturalists' Field Club, a County Councillor and a Justice of the Peace.

It was to the Woolhope Club that he presented, in 1921, a paper entitled 'Early British Trackways, Moats, Mounds, camp and sites'. In it he expounded his thesis that the British landscape was criss-crossed with a system of 'leys': straight lines which connected together ancient sites such as burial mounds, churches, hill-forts, ponds, beacons and standing stones. These leys had been developed as "straight trackways in prehistoric times in Britain".

In his subsequent book *The Old Straight Track* (1925), Watkins gives numerous examples and illustrations. One map extract in the book is marked with no fewer than seventeen straight lines drawn across the countryside in the Walton Basin of Radnorshire. Watkins describes as 'well authenticated' a ley which starts at Croft Ambrey Hill Fort, north-east of Leominster, and passes close by Hay, through the churches of Clyro and Llowes, to end, after 44 miles, at Fan Dringarth, a mountain summit in the Brecon Beacons. Llanthony Priory is described as "a favoured spot.... in the heart of the Black Mountains where primitive tracks and notches can well be studied."

> One Wednesday, towards the end of April, the bailiff sent him by train to Hereford, along with some lots of store-cattle, which were due to be sold at auction. Since the lots came up at eleven, the rest of the day was free. It was a very gloomy day and the clouds brushed low over the Cathedral tower. Lines of grey sleet smacked onto the pavements and rattled on the oilcloth hoods of the horse-cabs. When the sleet let up, he sauntered through the maze of lanes behind the Watkins Brewery.
>
> *On the Black Hill* – Chapter XXI

Alfred Watkins (photo from The Old Straight Track)

One of Watkins' maps, criss-crossed with 'leys'

To say that Watkins's views were unconventional is something of an understatement. He believed, for example, that the old straight tracks did not go round ponds, but through them. As evidence for this he cites the fact that "actual paved roads or causeways in the direction of the ley are sometimes found at the bottom of the ponds". Yet he is puzzled that "Most of these ponds seem to have one shelving edge, down which the causeway slopes, but the opposite end a perpendicular bank." One suspects that quite a brief conversation with a local livestock farmer might have resolved this conundrum.

Not everyone was immediately won over to the cause and in 1928 the *Journal of the Cambrian Archaeological Association* carried a scathing review of Watkins's *Ley Hunter's Manual*. A 1951 retrospective celebrating the centenary of the Woolhope Club pays glowing tribute to Alfred Watkins, but conspicuously omits to mention his old straight track:

> Another twentieth century stalwart was Alfred Watkins, F.R.P.S., the inventor of the photographic exposure meter and the tank development of negatives, and a constant contributor to the *Transactions* from 1890 until his death in 1935. His principal work was a volume on all the remains of preaching crosses in this county, with photographs of each, published by the club in 1930.

So that, you might think, would be that.

But no, Watkins had, and still has, his followers. With his emphasis on myths, legends, mysterious megaliths and ancient knowledge lost in the mists of time Watkins was a gift to the New Age counter culture of the 1960s and 70s. The fact that he had been rejected by mainstream archaeological establishment probably did him no harm either.

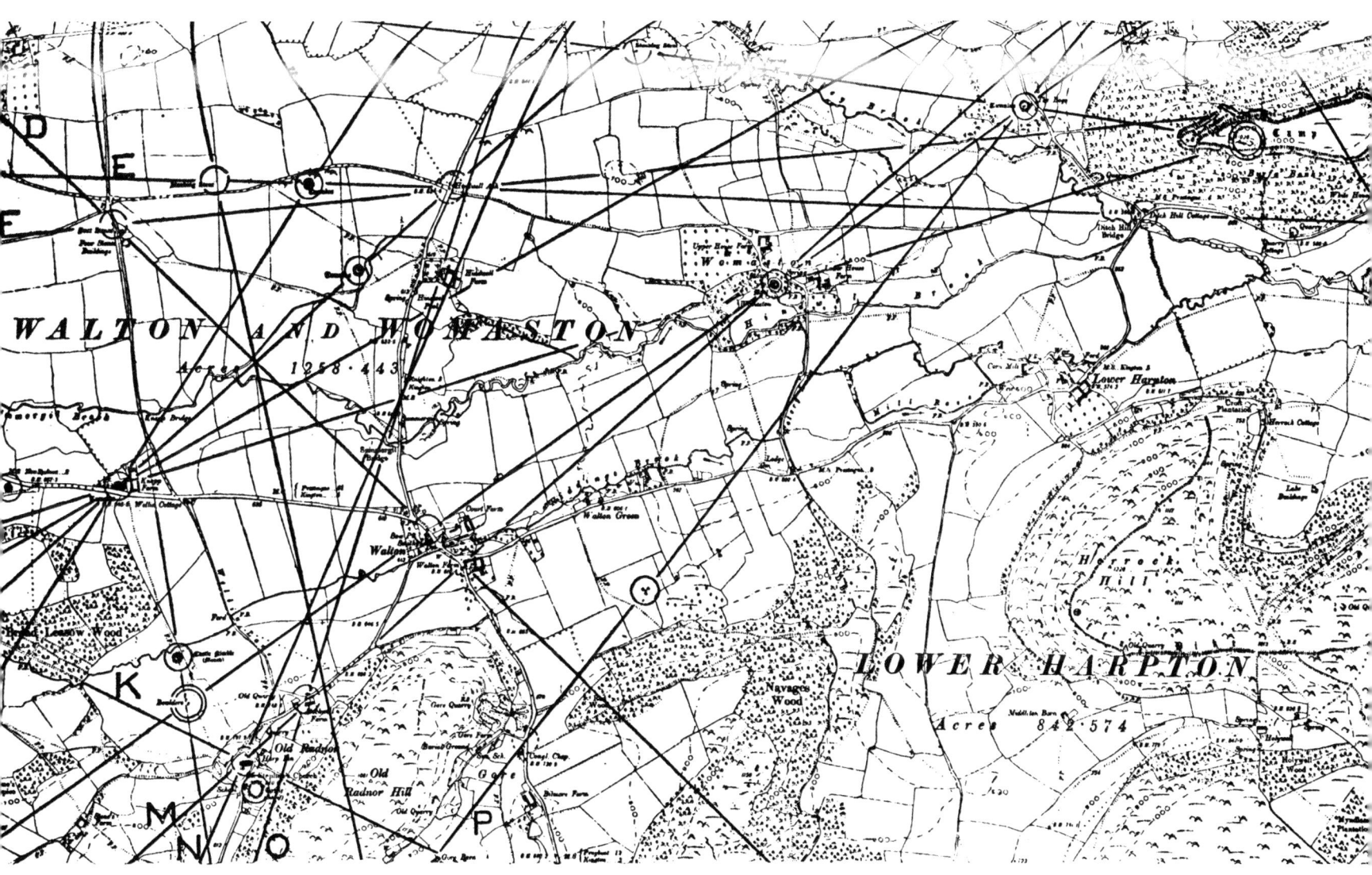

Our predilection for causal thinking exposes us to serious mistakes in evaluating the randomness of truly random events.

We are pattern seekers, believers in a coherent world, in which regularities appear not by accident but as a result of mechanical causality or someone's intention. We do not expect to see regularity produced by a random process, and when we detect what appears to be a rule, we quickly reject the idea that the process is truly random.

Daniel Kahneman in *Thinking, Fast and Slow* 2012

Janet and Colin Bord, authors of *Mysterious Britain* (1972) were in no doubt that Watkins was right:

> Although the existence of leys has been proved many times over, their real purpose is still uncertain. Alfred Watkins believed that they were early man's trackways…. Later researchers believe that this is only part of the answer, and that the leys may in fact follow invisible lines of power criss-crossing the countryside.

The Bords were certainly in tune with the times: their book was republished by Paladin in 1974, reset in 1975 reprinted in 1976 and again in 1977, the date of my copy. Fast forward another quarter century and still ley lines wouldn't lie down: 2003 brought *Ley Lines and Earth Energies: A Groundbreaking Exploration of the Earth's Natural Energy and How it Effects our Health* by David Cowan and Chris Arnold; followed in 2011 by *Sacred Network: Megaliths, Cathedrals, Ley Lines and the Power of Shared Consciousness* by Chris H. Hardy.

Meanwhile, back in Herefordshire, author Ron Shoesmith and local publisher Logaston Press have been doing their best to remind the world that there was a Watkins before ley lines. In 1990 they published *Alfred Watkins: A Herefordshire Man* and in 2012 *Alfred Watkins's Herefordshire – in his own words and photographs*. A noble effort.

On a ley? St. Michael's church, Clyro

The view from Arthur's Stone, one of Watkins' favourite sites, near Bredwardine

On the Trail of the Lonesome Pine

Alfred Watkins set much store by Scots pines (*Pinus sylvestris*, which both he and Kilvert called 'Scotch fir'), as waymarks. In this at least he is with the mainstream. In *The Drovers' Roads of Wales* Shirley Toulson says:

> In the open country, a farmer who wanted to let the drovers know that he was able to provide food, accommodation and grazing planted three Scots pines. These were visible at a great distance, and the drovers used them as waymarks. When they reached England, they found that groups of yew trees served the same purpose. These trees remain when all traces of the old inns or farms have disappeared, the stones having been used for other buildings.

Contributors to Richard Mabey's *Flora Britannica* tell several similar stories, to which he adds:

> there is no doubt that the drove-roads across the Welsh border carry one of the great concentrations of waymark pines..

Scots pines are well-suited to their task, being tall, having a distinctive silhouette and, since they are native only in Scotland, relatively unusual in this part of the country.

Scots Pines close to Offa's Dyke on Furrow Hill, with Radnor Forest and The Whimble beyond

Hay People – Sara Bowie, Gallery Owner

Sara Bowie is definitely New Hay, she even has a gallery, but there is a part of her that is Old Herefordshire too. Very much an Arts person Sara is an advisor to the Welsh Arts Council, through which she already knew Hay Festival Director Peter Florence when she moved to Hay in 1993. Sara became General Manager of the Festival for the next seven years, leaving shortly after her daughter India was born, in 1999. She then opened the Bowie Gallery by Hay's buttermarket. She is still very much involved in the Festival though, running the on-site gallery and sponsoring an event each year.

Sara was born in the former British colonial outpost of Aden, now part of Yemen, where her father was an RAF fighter pilot. But she is very proud of the fact that her great-grandfather was the first schoolmaster at Staunton-on-Wye in Herefordshire, down the river from Hay.

I asked Sara to name a favourite book, and she told me that when young she had been a huge fan of C.S. Lewis's Narnia books, which her older sister Alison used to read to her. Sara was so downcast when they reached the end of *The Last Battle* that Alison wrote another just for her. It was called *The Wind, the War and the Beginning* and was in typescript with hand-drawn illustrations. So that's the one she would take to her desert island.

Hay being a small town I should not have been surprised to learn that the late Martin Beales (see 'Dandelion Dead') had been Sara's solicitor.

> I sprang to my feet, my inert hand grasping my pistol, my mind paralysed by the dreadful shape which had sprung out upon us from the shadows of the fog. A hound it was, an enormous coal-black hound, but not such a hound as mortal eyes have ever seen. Fire burst from its open mouth, its eyes glowed with a smouldering glare, its muzzle and hackles and dewlap were outlined in flickering flame. Never in the delirious dream of a disordered brain could anything more savage, more appalling, more hellish, be conceived than that dark form and savage face which broke upon us out of the wall of fog.
>
> *The Hound of the Baskervilles*

Holmes and the Hound

Another name closely associated with Clyro, alongside Francis Kilvert, is that of the Baskerville family. The Baskervilles were local landowners for many generations and memorials to them can be seen at St Michael's Church. Not far from the church, in the centre of the village, is also the Baskerville Arms Hotel. Students of detective fiction may note that the Hotel's portico is adorned with a statue of a large dog, or hound, if you prefer. So, is this the Hound of the Baskervilles?

Sir Arthur Conan Doyle's novel *The Hound of the Baskervilles* was published in 1902. The story takes Sherlock Holmes to Dartmoor, and Baskerville Hall, the fictional ancient ancestral seat of the Baskerville family. For generations this family, many of whose members have died in mysterious circumstances, have been plagued by a giant dog:

> a foul thing, a great black beast, shaped like a hound, yet larger than any hound that ever mortal eye has rested upon.

But that was Dartmoor, which is in Devon, not Radnorshire, so surely it was not the Clyro Baskervilles?

Clyro Court

The Baskerville Arms Hotel

Perhaps we can learn more at Clyro Court, a mansion just south of the village, which was constructed in the mid-nineteenth century for Mr. Thomas Mynors Baskerville. Writing in the 1980s Richard Haslam confidently asserts that Conan Doyle resided at Clyro Court while writing the *The Hound of the Baskervilles*, whilst Mr David Hodby, the current owner, maintains that Sir Arthur was acquainted with the Baskerville family and was a regular visitor to the Court. Accordingly he now styles it the Baskerville Hall Hotel and his sign beside the Brecon Road features a gentleman in a deerstalker smoking a briar pipe. Perhaps there is a connection. But where did the dog come from?

The Baskerville Hall Hotel at Clyro Court

Did Sir Arthur Conan Doyle climb this staircase at Clyro Court?

Let us cross the border into Herefordshire, and Hergest Court, seat of the Vaughan family and famous among students of Welsh culture for the *Red Book of Hergest*. Hergest Court is about ten miles from Clyro, on the road to Kington and upon it centres a spooky local legend. The legend has it that centuries ago there lived at Hergest Court one Tomas ap Rosser, known as Black Vaughan, whose heinous deeds left a stain upon the family name and who has ever since been associated with a ghostly hound which haunts Hergest Ridge and the neighbouring hills of Herefordshire and Radnorshire. In her book *Arthur, Louise and the True Hound of the Baskervilles* Margaret Newman Turner gives an account of the legend which is strikingly similar in many details to that of the Hound of the Baskervilles as presented by Conan Doyle.

Furthermore Mrs. Newman Turner reports that Louise, the first Mrs Arthur Conan Doyle, was owner of two farms in the close vicinity of Clyro: Clyro Bettws, and Whitehall Farm, which after her death were sold by Sir Arthur to the Baskerville estate. Evidence of this exists in the form of a title deed preserved in the archives of Powys County Council on which appears the signature of Sir Arthur Conan Doyle, alongside that of R.H. Baskerville.

So it is certainly true to say that Conan Doyle was acquainted with Clyro but he declined to acknowledge any connection between the village and his famous story. In a letter to Margaret Newman Turner's grandfather, Mr Cecil P. Turner of Kington, he states that he had no particular place in mind when he wrote it.

So there you have it.

Hergest Court

Haunted: Hergest Ridge, Kington

Hay People – Josie Pearson, Paralympian

I took this picture of Josie Pearson for Hay's local paper, the *Brecon and Radnor Express*, when she was the guest of honour turning on Hay's Christmas lights in 2012. As you can see she is a popular woman.

2012 was big year for Josie, the year she finally achieved the success she had sought in no fewer than six different sports. The *Guardian* of 8th September 2012 reports that Josie tried showjumping, dressage, wheelchair rugby, wheelchair racing and club throwing before finally winning gold in the discus at the London paralympics. She is a lot more energetic than I was at that age (26).

As a gold medallist Josie, who lives in Cusop, has had her own stamp produced by the Royal Mail and has been celebrated in Hay too, where a postbox in the town was painted gold in her honour.

Josie's neck was broken in a car crash when she was a teenager, since when she has been able to move only her arms. The *Guardian* article describes her as being "about as severely disabled as any competitor who has been into the stadium this week" and quotes her as saying "I can't emphasise enough how beneficial sport has been. It has given me back my independence, which you think you're never going to get when you're lying in hospital."

An Excursion with The Woolhope Naturalists' Field Club

To dip into the transactions of the The Woolhope Naturalists' Field Club for 1911 is to take an excursion to another age. An age when gentlemen wore waistcoats, ladies wore corsets and the two mingled infrequently.

Founded in 1851 the Woolhope Club still keeps a very fine library in Hereford, and it has paid many visits to Hay and district. In 1911 their first field meeting of the year, on 30th May, began at Hay. The party arrived by train from Hereford for an exploration of Clyro, Rhosgoch and Painscastle. A nice description of their journey from Hay to Clyro is given opposite.

Later, dinner was taken at Hay's Crown Hotel, where the list of members present includes President Mr E. Cambridge Phillips, followed by his Honour Judge Ingham, Lt. Col. J.E.R. Campbell, seventeen clergymen, three doctors and twenty-two gentlemen, including Alfred Watkins. Guests include Mr J.M. Hutchinson of Natal and Mr W. Carman of the *Hereford Times*. No ladies are mentioned.

The *Transactions* themselves are beautifully typeset and printed, and bound between embossed hard covers. From the 1920s onwards the *Transactions* are less lavishly produced, but the 1908-11 volume is a lovely book to handle. It is full, too, of fascinating little details, giving insights into the times. At the front of the volume the rules of the club are enumerated. Rule IX reads as follows:

> That all candidates for membership shall be proposed and seconded by existing members, either verbally or in writing, at any meeting of the club, and shall be eligible to be balloted for at the next meeting, provided there be FIVE members present; one black ball in three to exclude.

Woolhope Naturalists' Field Club.

First Field Meeting, Tuesday, May 30th, 1911.

WILD WALES.

VISIT TO RHOSGOCH AND PAINSCASTLE.

INTERESTING INCIDENTS.

Not for many years have the members of the Woolhope Naturralists' Field Club toured the wild and charming surroundings of Rhosgoch and Painscastle, and there was small cause for wonder that the field meeting of Tuesday to this district was so largely attended on the occasion of the first field day of the season. The visit was made by kind permission of Captain Walter de Winton.

The major portion of the party, numbering about 60, boarded the 9.22 a.m. Midland train, on which compartments were set apart for the club, at Barrs Court Station, Hereford, and other members were picked up en route to Hay, where on their arrival they were met by this year's President, Mr. E. Cambridge Phillips. The President, unfortunately, was unable to accompany the members on their tour owing to a professional engagement, and Mr. Henry Southall, of Ross, acted as president during the itinerary. Conveyances having met the party at the station, they proceeded over the Wye Bridge, where toll was demanded and promptly paid—fourpence for each horse and a halfpenny for each person—to Clyro. The weather was glorious, a cool breeze tempering what would otherwise have been the hottest day of the year. There was every promise of the atmospheric conditions continuing, and in this the party was not disappointed. At Clyro, the road to the right, past the Baskerville Arms, was taken, followed by a turn to the left past Cwm Evan Gwyn. Clyro was traversed on foot, many of the travellers felt constrained to remove their jackets, and some their waistcoats as well, during the ascent of this steep and long hill. Once more the conveyances were boarded, and the famous Rhosgoch bog was reached at the eastern end, where there is a Castle tump and some tumuli near Doleycanney. Driving along the northern side

> ...Give me leave
> To tell you once again that at my birth
> The front of heaven was full of fiery shapes
> The goats ran from the mountains, and the herds
> Were strangely clamorous to the frighted fields
> These signs have mark'd me extraordinary;
> And all the courses of my life do show
> I am not in the roll of common men.
>
> Shakespeare's 'Owen Glendower', in *Henry IV, Part I*, Act III, Scene I

In search of Owain Glyndŵr

Early in the preparation of this book I hoped that I might find favour with a Welsh publisher, and in pursuit of this end I decided that I would weave into my work the story of Owain Glyndŵr, the fifteenth century warrior Prince who, one biographer said, "may with propriety be called the father of modern Welsh nationalism."

Lucky for me, I thought, that Glyndŵr (known to the English as Owen Glendower) conquered both Hay and Hereford in 1404 during his campaign against the English King Henry IV. Luckier still that he is widely believed to be buried in as many as four places in Herefordshire, two of them within a stone's throw of Hay. The deeper I dug the more I liked the story, and the pictures, so I decided to stick with it.

Owain Glyndŵr's rebellion began in North Wales in 1400 and his most famous victory over the English took place just 16 miles north of Hay at the battle of Pilleth, on 22nd June 1402. Here he defeated the forces of the powerful Marcher Lord Edmund Mortimer, of Wigmore. Mortimer, captured by Glyndŵr, then changed sides, made an alliance with his captor and even married one of his daughters.

Shakespeare portrays both Glyndŵr and Mortimer in *Henry IV, Part I*. In Act III, Scene I he has them in heated negotiation with Hotspur, son of Henry Percy, Earl of Northumberland. Confident of eventual victory over the king, they pore over a map, dividing up England and Wales between themselves and arguing over the course of the River Trent. In real life the result was the Tripartite Identure of 1405.

Pilleth

Snow on the mass grave at Bryn Glas

Many books have been written on Owain Glyndŵr, but, shopping local, I have taken as my guide Elizabeth Dunn, writing in the *Transactions of the Radnorshire Society* in 1967. She reports that early in the twentieth century local landowner Sir Richard Green-Price discovered human bones on Bryn Glâs, the hill above St Mary's Church at Pilleth, and planted a square patch of fir trees to mark the spot where he presumed the dead of the battle to lie buried. The trees are now a local landmark and the site is signposted from the B4356.

After Pilleth, Dunn writes:

> It now looked as though he would triumph completely. He was in alliance with two powerful and ambitious magnates, and he had received a modicum of support from the French King. But Glyndŵr had been too successful. He had given Henry IV too much to worry about. He was no longer a petty Welsh rebel, but a potential maker and destroyer of Kings.

After his eventual defeat Glyndŵr became a fugitive, and it seems that he was never found, a fact which has of course only enhanced his reputation down the centuries. In the sixteenth century Shakespeare wrote about Owen Glendower, in the nineteenth Kilvert did, in late twentieth an underground group of militant Welsh nationalists adopted the name 'Meibion Glyndŵr' (Sons of Glyndŵr) and went about the countryside burning English-owned holiday cottages. In the 1970s Powys County Council, looking to name a new long-distance walking route around mid-Wales, hit upon 'Glyndŵr's Way', and in 2000 the Owain Glyndŵr Society, celebrated the 600th anniversary of his revolt.

St Mary's Church, Pilleth

Monnington Court, Vowchurch

And not only has Glyndŵr's reputation survived, it has spread. In 2012, at the Offa's Dyke Centre in Knighton, I met Jaime Ong, an English teacher from the Phillipines, who, having read about Glyndŵr in *Henry IV, Part I*, and learned that he had put Knighton to the torch, was paying us a visit to find out more about him.

But to return to the burial places. Elizabeth Dunn attributed the unusual number of possible sites to the fact that Glyndŵr seems to have had many daughters:

> one, probably Alice, married John Scudamore, of the famous Scudamore family of Herefordshire. Another one, perhaps Elizabeth, Catherine, Jane or Janet, married Edmund Mortimer. Another daughter probably married Sir John Hanmer of Herefordshire: and it was strongly believed in the sixteenth century that one daughter had married Sir John Croft of Croft's Castle, Herefordshire.

The confusion is not eased by the fact that there are two houses called Monnington Court in Herefordshire, and that both have been connected with relatives of Glyndŵr. Colin Lewis, writing in 2006, lists the four possible locations as Monnington-on-Wye, Monnington Court at Vowchurch, Croft Castle, and Kentchurch. Dunn refers to Sir J.E. Lloyd who, in his 1931 biography, said that Glyndŵr died at Monnington Straddel, at the home of his daughter, Alice Scudamore, and was buried in the adjacent churchyard.

Jaime and Cynthia Ong researching Glyndŵr

Monnington Court Monnington-on-Wye

This would appear to be a vote for Monnington Court, Vowchurch, which is immediately adjacent to Monnington Straddel. However my own researches find that there is, at least today, no churchyard adjacent, or even near, to this Monnington Court. The other Monnington Court, at Monnington-on-Wye, however, does have a churchyard next door, and one which was almost certainly there in Glyndŵr's time.

On turning to Francis Kilvert I found that Monnington-on-Wye had his firm vote. He was there on 5th April 1875 and wrote of:

> Monnington Court House, where the aunt of Owen Glendower lived.

And the following day:

> Hard by the Church porch and on the western side of it I saw what I knew must be the grave of Owen Glendower. It is a flat stone of whitish grey shaped like a rude obelisk figure, sunk deep into the ground in the middle of an oblong patch of earth from which the turf has been pared away, and, alas, smashed into several fragments. And here in the little Herefordshire churchyard within hearing of the rushing of the Wye and close under the shadow of the old grey church the strong wild heart, still now, has rested by the ancient home and roof tree of his kindred since he fell asleep there more than four hundred years ago. It is a quiet peaceful spot.

Clearly this merited further investigation. A trip to Monnington-on-Wye was called for.

Glyndŵr's Way

Monnington-on-Wye

Sunday, 23 April 1876

One of the quiet peaceful Monnington Sundays. I like a Sunday at Monnington, it is so calm and so serene. There is no hurry, no crowd, no confusion, no noise.

Kilvert's Diary

An Excursion to Monnington-on-Wye

It was a Friday, and January, when I took my copy of Kilvert to Monnington-on-Wye, but otherwise it was just as he described: calm and serene, with no hurry, no crowd, no confusion, no noise. Hardly anyone about at all in fact. An abundance of wildlife though. Monnington is surrounded on three sides by cider orchards and these were alive with fieldfares, calling continuously. From time to time a buzzard joined in, circling somewhere nearby and mewing loudly. Also out of sight, toward the river, a flock of starlings was chattering quietly away. But, better than any of this, in the churchyard, in the sun, there were snowdrops, my first of the year. So I took some pictures of those, as I always feel compelled to do, and then went looking for evidence of Owain Glyndŵr.

Of this I regret to report I could find none at all. Hard by the Church porch and on the western side there were a number of flat stone graves, but none which seemed to match Kilvert's description. In the church I found some information about Kilvert but no reference to Glyndŵr, so I sought consolation instead in comparing other features of Kilvert's Monnington with the Monnington of today.

Here I enjoyed more success. The 'Scotch firs' of Monnington Walk are still there, and a commemorative plaque informed me that they make an avenue a mile long, first

A fieldfare feasting on fallen apples

First snowdrops

When I awoke a wood pigeon was crooning from the trees near the house and the early morning sunshine glinted upon the red boles of the gigantic Scotch firs in Monnington Walk.

Kilvert's Diary – 6th April 1875

planted in 1641. The avenue is now part of the Wye Valley Walk, by which Kilvert, if he were alive today, could walk all the way back to Hay. (You could too, it's about ten miles.) Monnington Court, Kilvert's 'old grey mansion of the Glendowers' is still there, and the church of St Mary may well be exactly as it was in the diarist's day. Writing in 1963 Nikolaus Pevsner described it thus:

> Unbuttressed Perp★ W tower with very large battlements pierced by cruciform arrow slits. The rest of the church dates from 1679 and is uncommonly complete, in structure and furnishings. It was built for Uvedall Tomkyns. The plan is entirely the medieval one of nave and chancel.

Even Pevsner's description is half-a-century old though, so imagine my surprise and delight on finding, in January 2013, that the church still appears to be lit by oil lamps. If that is the case then I think we can safely assume that not much else will have changed here since the swinging sixties. It is a real gem, go and see it, but be advised: Monnington is a small hamlet of narrow lanes with not so much as a lay-by for parking. I took my chances with a rather iffy grass verge. There's still the Wye Valley Walk though!

> ★Perp = Perpendicular Gothic: an architectural style which implies construction between the mid fourteenth and mid sixteenth century. So Owain Glyndŵr could conceivably have seen the tower of St Mary's under construction when he visited Monnington Court in the 1400s.

The west tower at St Mary's

Monnington Walk

Hay is asleep in August after the second-hand bookshops have closed. Those who have walked over the ridge are soon asleep too.

Jasper Rees in *Bred of Heaven*

An Excursion along the Offa's Dyke Path

I wonder if I could trouble you for some advice. I am planning to walk as much of Offa's Dyke as possible this year but do not have quite enough time to do the full stretch. I understand it takes about twelve days and realistically I have nine days, perhaps nine and a half if I start at lunchtime from Chepstow on, ten at a push. Are there two days on the walk that are slightly less exciting that I could afford to miss out?
   (I should add that I am writing a book about Wales and Welshness, and walking Offa's Dyke will form one chapter. I am also writing an article about the walk for the *Daily Mail* and have been in touch with Visit Wales and the PR company in London about it.)

Best wishes,
Jasper Rees

So began, in 2010, an extended correspondence between myself and this Jasper Rees about his proposed expedition along the Offa's Dyke Path. It was not by any means the first enquiry of this sort I had received and to be honest I was not entirely convinced by Rees's literary aspirations, but I humoured him and answered his questions as best I could.

Then *Bred of Heaven*, by one Jasper Rees, turned up as Book of the Week on BBC Radio 4. So that's how much I know about literary talent.

Offa's Dyke Path fingerpost

Offa's Dyke in south Shropshire

On the other hand I can claim know a bit about the Offa's Dyke Path, for it was the Path which first brought me to Hay, in 1987, coincidentally the year of the first Hay Festival. I walked from Hay to Knighton in March of that year in preparation for the job interview which led to my becoming the Offa's Dyke Path Officer for the next eighteen years. It was a memorable trip. There had been a considerable fall of snow which was followed by days of clear skies with frost and sun. I found myself walking in brilliant early Spring weather over snow-clad hills, wading through the occasional drift to reach a stile in a sheltered field corner. I became, and remain, a big fan.

The Offa's Dyke Path goes right through the middle of Hay, entering the town from the south via Cusop Dingle, passing close by the castle and the clock and leaving, north-bound, via the the Wye Bridge. South of Hay the Path traverses the Black Mountains, following the crest of Hatterrall Ridge for ten miles before it descends to the Vale of Usk near Abergavenny. If you pick the right day it is a spectacular walk with views west into Wales and the Brecon Beacons; and east across Herefordshire to the Malvern and Cotswold Hills. If you pick the wrong day, well, you'll still get plenty of fresh air.

The border between England and Wales also follows the Hatterrall Ridge for a consider-able distance, giving rise to a widespread misconception that Offa's Dyke, the ancient border earthwork, does too. So some definitions may be helpful here.

Offa's Dyke is a 1,200 year-old bank-and-ditch earthwork generally believed to have been constructed in the late eighth century AD on the orders of Offa, the Saxon King

The Offa's Dyke Path on Hay Bluff, with the Hatterall Ridge beyond

of Mercia to mark, and perhaps defend, the western edge of his territory. This was before either England or Wales existed as unified countries but the Dyke was later to become the symbolic boundary between the two. About 80 miles of the Dyke can still be seen today, the greater part of this being between Kington in Herefordshire and Wrexham in North Wales. In Herefordshire south of Kington only odd fragments of the Dyke are still visible. Of these the nearest to Hay is just beyond Staunton-on-Wye and runs north, on private land, from the A438 Hereford Road, to Garnon's Hill.

The modern border between England and Wales was defined in the Act of Settlement of 1536. Some parts of this border still follow Offa's Dyke, but mainly it is marked out, as boundaries often are, by natural features of the landscape. So south of Hay Bluff the border follows the mountain ridge, in the town itself the Dulas Brook and then, downstream from Hay, the River Wye.

The Offa's Dyke Path is a twentieth century invention. Opened in 1971 it is one of the fifteen National Trails in England and Wales. This National Trail runs 177 miles from Sedbury Cliffs, on the Severn Estuary, to Prestatyn on the North Wales coast. Much, but by no means all, of it follows King Offa's earthwork. In some cases, as in the vicinity of Hay, there was not enough Dyke to follow; in others, particularly in the north around Wrexham, it was deemed more important to find an attractive walking route than to meticulously follow in Offa's footsteps.

Postscript: To this day the Welsh word for the English is 'Saeson', which literally means 'Saxons'.

On the Offa's Dyke Path

Saxon invasion? A group of German journalists sample the Offa's Dyke Path and explore their inner Welshness at Hay Bridge

The Kissing Bridge

If you walk south from Hay Castle on the Offa's Dyke Path you will, before long come to a footbridge over a small stream on the edge of Cusop Dingle. I rebuilt this bridge in the late 1980s, assisted by two workmen and a JCB from Powys County Council. One day while we were working a gent from the town came along and told us a little story. He said that his wife, who was a local girl, had told him that this bridge had always been known as the Kissing Bridge, because courting couples from the town would walk out this way and linger over the stream.

So when I came to making the handrails for the bridge I engraved that name on them, along with the Welsh translation, 'Y Pont Gusanu'.

I went back to the bridge in the autumn of 2012 and was pleased to find not only that the name was still there, but that the bridge was still firm, and wearing well after more than twenty years. Have a look and see what you think. Take a friend.

The Brecon Beacons

Built right up to the English border Hay is, some might say, only just in Wales. But in Wales it is. And the town is also in the Brecon Beacons National Park, just, forming its far northernmost tip.

The Brecon Beacons proper actually occupy the western half of the 'Park', around the town of Brecon itself. Nearer to hand are the Black Mountains, which include Hay Bluff and, adjacent to it, the picturesquely-named Lord Hereford's Knob. These mountains, like Hay, press hard against the border: their steep eastern flank is actually within Herefordshire.

British National Parks are not remote wilderness areas like their American counterparts; they are very much inhabited and farmed; but the Brecon Beacons are by tradition the lungs of the famous South Wales mining valleys. A long-established resort for ramblers, cyclists and charabancs they were an obvious candidate when the first list of proposed National Parks was drawn up in the mid-twentieth century. So you won't encounter elk or grizzley bears in the Brecon Beacons, but you are very likely to hear the familiar South Wales accent, perhaps from the family of a former miner, having a day out in the hills. Not to mention the Welsh language itself of course, widely spoken in the west of the Park.

At 886 metres (2,900 feet) Pen y fan is the highest point in the Brecon Beacons. Its summit is a flat slab of bare sandstone, which gives the mountain a distinctive profile, recognisable from as far as forty miles away. On any half-decent day you will have a fine view of Pen y fan and the Beacons from the car park at the stone circle below Hay Bluff.

A snow shower approaches Cribyn, in the Brecon Beacons

Bibliography

Bord, Janet and Colin: *Mysterious Britain* (Garnstone Press, 1972)
Burnham, Helen: *A Guide to Ancient and Historic Wales – Clwyd and Powys* (Cadw – Welsh Historic Monuments/HMSO, 1995)
Carter, Harold: *The Towns of Wales* (University of Wales Press, 1965-6)
Chatwin, Bruce: *On the Black Hill* (Jonathan Cape, 1982)
Conan Doyle, Arthur: *The Hound of the Baskervilles* (George Newnes, 1902)
Dugdale, William: *Monasticon Anglicanum* English translation (from Latin) 1693.
Dunn, Elizabeth: 'Owain Glyndŵr in Radnorshire' *Transactions of the Radnorshire Society* Vol. XXXVII, 1967
Gill, Eric: *Autobiography* (Jonathan Cape, 1940)
Gill, M.A.V.: 'Three Documents in the Parish Archives of the Wye Valley Group' *Transactions of the Radnorshire Society* Vol LXXVII, 2007
Godwin, Fay and Toulson, Shirley: *The Drovers' Roads of Wales* (Wildwood House, 1977)
Haslam, Richard: *The Buildings of Wales – Powys* (Penguin, 1979)
Hay Chamber of Trade: *Hay Holiday Guide Book* (c.1925)
Jones, Anthony: *Welsh Chapels* (National Museum of Wales, 1984)
Kahneman, Daniel: *Thinking, Fast and Slow* (Penguin, 2012)
Kilvert, Francis: *Kilvert's Diary 1870-79*, Ed. William Plomer (Jonathan Cape, 1944)
Lewis, Colin: *Herefordshire – the Welsh Connection* (Gwasg Carreg Gwalch, 2006)
Mabey, Richard: *Food for Free* (Wm. Collins & Sons, 1972)
Mabey, Richard: *Flora Britannica* (Sinclair-Stevenson, 1996)
Pevsner, Nikolaus: *The Buildings of England – Herefordshire* (Penguin Books, 1963)
Radnorshire Society, Transactions, various volumes from the Frank Noble Library at the Offa's Dyke Centre, Knighton
Rees, Jasper: *Bred of Heaven* (Profile Books, 2011)
Rowley, Trevor: *The Landscape of the Welsh Marches* (Michael Joseph, 1986)
Sellar, W.C. and Yeatman, R.J.: *1066 and ALL THAT* (Methuen & Co. Ltd., 1930)
Shoesmith, Ron and Jennifer: *Alfred Watkins' Herefordshire* (Logaston Press, 2012)
Turner, Margaret Newman: *Arthur, Louise and the True Hound of the Baskervilles* (Logaston Press, 2010)

Vaughan-Thomas, Wynford & Llewelyn, Alun: *The Shell Guide to Wales* (Michael Joseph, 1969)
Watkins, Alfred: *The Old Straight Track* (Methuen, 1925)
White, Rev. Gilbert: *The Natural History of Selborne* (1788)
Wilson, A.N.: *The Victorians* (Hutchinson, 2002)
Woolhope Naturalists Field Club, Transactions, various volumes from the Frank Noble Library at the Offa's Dyke Centre, Knighton
Maesyronnen – a short history and description, author unidentified (2008)